The Constitution of
The State of North Dakota:
A Quick Reference Guide

Bootblack Budget Books
Copyright 2018 ©
ISBN-13: 978-1720462002
ISBN-10: 1720462003

Contents:

Preamble – Page 3

Article I: Declaration of Rights – Page 4

Article II: Elective Franchise – Page 13

Article III: Powers Reserved To The People – Page 14

Article IV: Legislative Branch – Page 18

Article V: Executive Branch – Page 24

Article VI: Judicial Branch – Page 29

Article VII: Political Subdivisions – Page 33

Article VIII: Education – Page 36

Article IX: Trust Lands – Page 42

Article X: Finance and Public Debt – Page 51

Article XI: General Provisions – Page 63

Article XII: Corporations Other Than Municipal – Page 69

Article XIII: Compact With The United States – Page 71

Transition Schedule – Page 72

PREAMBLE

We, the people of North Dakota, grateful to Almighty God for the blessings of civil and religious liberty, do ordain and establish this constitution.

ARTICLE I: DECLARATION OF RIGHTS

Section 1. All individuals are by nature equally free and independent and have certain inalienable rights, among which are those of enjoying and defending life and liberty; acquiring, possessing and protecting property and reputation; pursuing and obtaining safety and happiness; and to keep and bear arms for the defense of their person, family, property, and the state, and for lawful hunting, recreational, and other lawful purposes, which shall not be infringed.

Section 2. All political power is inherent in the people. Government is instituted for the protection, security and benefit of the people, and they have a right to alter or reform the same whenever the public good may require.

Section 3. The free exercise and enjoyment of religious profession and worship, without discrimination or preference shall be forever guaranteed in this state, and no person shall be rendered incompetent to be a witness or juror on account of his opinion on matters of religious belief; but the liberty of conscience hereby secured shall not be so construed as to excuse acts of licentiousness, or justify practices inconsistent with the peace or safety of this state.

Section 4. Every man may freely write, speak and publish his opinions on all subjects, being responsible for the abuse of that privilege. In all civil and criminal trials for libel the truth may be given in evidence, and shall be a sufficient defense when the matter is published with good motives and for justifiable ends; and the jury shall have the same power of giving a general verdict as in other cases; and in all indictments or informations for libels the jury shall have the right to determine the law and the facts under the direction of the court as in other cases.

Section 5. The citizens have a right, in a peaceable manner, to assemble together for the common good, and to apply to those invested with the powers of government for the redress of grievances, or for other proper purposes, by petition, address or remonstrance.

Section 6. Neither slavery nor involuntary servitude, unless for the punishment of crime, shall ever be tolerated in this state.

Section 7. Every citizen of this state shall be free to obtain employment wherever possible, and any person, corporation, or agent thereof, maliciously interfering or hindering in any way, any citizen from obtaining or enjoying employment already obtained, from any other corporation or person, shall be deemed guilty of a misdemeanor.

Section 8. The right of the people to be secure in their persons, houses, papers and effects, against unreasonable searches and seizures shall not be violated; and no warrant shall issue but upon probable cause, supported by oath or affirmation, particularly describing the place to be searched and the persons and things to be seized. Section 9. All courts shall be open, and every man for any injury done him in his lands, goods, person or reputation shall have remedy by due process of law, and right and justice administered without sale, denial or delay. Suits may be brought against the state in such manner, in such courts, and in such cases, as the legislative assembly may, by law, direct.

Section 10. Until otherwise provided by law, no person shall, for a felony, be proceeded against criminally, otherwise than by indictment, except in cases arising in the land or naval forces, or in the militia when in actual service in time of war or public danger. In all other cases, offenses shall be prosecuted criminally by indictment or information. The legislative assembly may change, regulate or abolish the grand jury system.

Section 11. All persons shall be bailable by sufficient sureties, unless for capital offenses when the proof is evident or the presumption great. Excessive bail shall not be required, nor excessive fines imposed, nor shall cruel or unusual punishments be inflicted. Witnesses shall not be unreasonably detained, nor be confined in any room where criminals are actually imprisoned.

Section 12. In criminal prosecutions in any court whatever, the party accused shall have the right to a speedy and public trial; to have the process of the court to compel the attendance of witnesses in his behalf; and to appear and defend in person and with counsel. No person shall be twice put in jeopardy for the same offense, nor be compelled in any criminal case to be a witness against himself, nor be deprived of life, liberty or property without due process of law.

Section 13. The right of trial by jury shall be secured to all, and remain inviolate. A person accused of a crime for which he may be confined for a period of more than one year has the right of trial by a jury of twelve. The legislative assembly may determine the size of the jury for all other cases, provided that the jury consists of at least six members. All verdicts must be unanimous.

Section 14. The privilege of the writ of habeas corpus shall not be suspended unless, when in case of rebellion or invasion, the public safety may require.

Section 15. No person shall be imprisoned for debt unless upon refusal to deliver up his estate for the benefit of his creditors, in such manner as shall be prescribed by law; or in cases of tort; or where there is strong presumption of fraud.

Section 16. Private property shall not be taken or damaged for public use without just compensation having been first made to, or paid into court for the owner, unless the owner chooses to accept annual payments as may be provided for by law. No right of way shall be appropriated to the use of any corporation until full compensation therefor be first made in money or ascertained and paid into court for the owner, unless the owner chooses annual payments as may be provided by law, irrespective of any benefit from any improvement proposed by such corporation. Compensation shall be ascertained by a jury, unless a jury be waived. When the state or any of its departments, agencies or political subdivisions seeks to acquire right of way, it may take possession upon making an offer to purchase and by depositing the amount of such offer with the clerk of the district court of the county wherein the right of way is located. The clerk shall immediately notify the owner of such deposit. The owner may thereupon appeal to the court in the manner provided by law, and may have a jury trial, unless a jury be waived, to determine the damages, which damages the owner may choose to accept in annual payments as may be provided for by law. Annual payments shall not be subject to escalator clauses but may be supplemented by interest earned. For purposes of this section, a public use or a public purpose does not include public benefits of economic development, including an increase in tax base, tax revenues, employment, or general economic health. Private property shall not be taken for the use of, or ownership by, any private individual or entity, unless that property is necessary for conducting a common carrier or utility business.

Section 17. Treason against the state shall consist only in levying war against it, adhering to its enemies or giving them aid and comfort. No person shall be convicted of treason unless on the evidence of two witnesses to the same overt act, or confession in open court.

Section 18. No bill of attainder, ex post facto law, or law impairing the obligations of contracts shall ever be passed.

Section 19. The military shall be subordinate to the civil power. No standing army shall be maintained by this state in time of peace, and no soldiers shall, in time of peace, be quartered in any house without the consent of the owner; nor in time of war, except in the manner prescribed by law.

Section 20. To guard against transgressions of the high powers which we have delegated, we declare that everything in this article is excepted out of the general powers of government and shall forever remain inviolate.

Section 21. No special privileges or immunities shall ever be granted which may not be altered, revoked or repealed by the legislative assembly; nor shall any citizen or class of citizens be granted privileges or immunities which upon the same terms shall not be granted to all citizens.

Section 22. All laws of a general nature shall have a uniform operation.

Section 23. The state of North Dakota is an inseparable part of the American union and the Constitution of the United States is the supreme law of the land.

Section 24. The provisions of this constitution are mandatory and prohibitory unless, by express words, they are declared to be otherwise.

Section 25.

1. To preserve and protect the right of crime victims to justice, to ensure crime victims a meaningful role throughout the criminal and juvenile justice systems, and to ensure that crime victims rights and interests are respected and protected by law in a manner no less vigorous than the protections afforded to criminal defendants and delinquent children, all victims shall be entitled to the following rights, beginning at the time of their victimization:

a. The right to be treated with fairness and respect for the victim's dignity.

b. The right to be free from intimidation, harassment, and abuse.

c. The right to be reasonably protected from the accused and any person acting on behalf of the accused.

d. The right to have the safety and welfare of the victim and the victim's family considered when setting bail or making release decisions.

e. The right to prevent the disclosure of information or records that could be used to locate or harass the victim or the victim's family, or which could disclose confidential or privileged information about the victim, and to be notified of any request for such information or records.

f. The right to privacy, which includes the right to refuse an interview, deposition, or other discovery request made by the defendant, the defendant's attorney, or any person acting on behalf of the defendant, and to set reasonable conditions on the conduct of any such interaction to which the victim consents. Nothing in this section shall abrogate a defendant's sixth amendment rights under the Constitution of the United States nor diminish the state's disclosure obligations to a defendant.

g. The right to reasonable, accurate, and timely notice of, and to be present at, all proceedings involving the criminal or delinquent conduct, including release, plea, sentencing, adjudication, and disposition, and any proceeding during which a right of the victim is implicated.

h. The right to be promptly notified of any release or escape of the accused.

i. The right to be heard in any proceeding involving release, plea, sentencing, adjudication, disposition, or parole, and any proceeding during which a right of the victim is implicated.

j. The right, upon request, to confer with the attorney for the government.

k. The right to provide information regarding the impact of the offender's conduct on the victim and the victim's family to the individual responsible for conducting any presentence or disposition investigation or compiling any presentence investigation report or recommendation regarding, and to have any such information considered in any sentencing or disposition recommendations.

l. The right, upon request, to receive a copy of any report or record relevant to the exercise of a victim's right, except for those portions made confidential by law or unless a court determines disclosure would substantially interfere with the investigation of a case, and to receive a copy of any presentence report or plan of disposition when available to the defendant or delinquent child.

m. The right, upon request, to the prompt return of the victim's property when no longer needed as evidence in the case.

n. The right to full and timely restitution in every case and from each offender for all losses suffered by the victim as a result of the criminal or delinquent conduct. All monies and property collected from any person who has been ordered to make restitution shall be first applied to the restitution owed to the victim before paying any amounts owed to the government.

o. The right to proceedings free from unreasonable delay, and to a prompt and final conclusion of the case and any related post-judgment proceedings.

p. The right, upon request, to be informed of the conviction, adjudication, sentence, disposition, place, and time of incarceration, detention, or other disposition of the offender, any scheduled release date of the offender, and the release of or the escape by the offender from custody or commitment.

q. The right, upon request, to be informed in a timely manner of all post-judgment processes and procedures, to participate in such processes and procedures, to provide information to the release authority to be considered before any release decision is made, and to be notified of any release decision regarding the offender. The parole authority shall extend the right to be heard to any person harmed by the offender.

r. The right, upon request, to be informed in a timely manner of any pardon, commutation, reprieve, or expungement procedures, to provide information to the governor, the court, any pardon board, and other authority in these procedures, and to have that information considered before a decision is made, and to be notified of such decision in advance of any release of the offender.

s. The right to be informed of these rights, and to be informed that victims can seek the advice of an attorney with respect to their rights. This information shall be made available to the general public and provided to all crime victims in what is referred to as a Marsy's card.

2. The victim, the retained attorney of the victim, a lawful representative of the victim, or the attorney for the government upon request of the victim may assert and seek enforcement of the rights enumerated in this section and any other right afforded to a victim by law in any trial or appellate court, or before any other authority with jurisdiction over the case, as a matter of right. The court or other authority with jurisdiction shall act promptly on such a request, ensuring that no right is deprived without due process of law, and affording a remedy by due course of law for the violation of any right. The reasons for any decision regarding disposition of a victim's right shall be clearly stated on the record.

3. The granting of these rights to victims shall not be construed to deny or disparage other rights possessed by victims. All provisions of this section apply throughout criminal and juvenile justice processes and are self-enabling. This section does not create any cause of action for damages against the state, any political subdivision of the state, any officer, employee, or agent of the state or of any of its political subdivisions, or any officer or employee of the court.

4. As used in this section, a "victim" is a person who suffers direct or threatened physical, psychological, or financial harm as a result of the commission or attempted commission of a crime or delinquent act or against whom the crime or delinquent act is committed. If a victim is deceased, incompetent, incapacitated, or a minor, the victim's spouse, parent, grandparent, child, sibling, grandchild, or guardian, and any person with a relationship to the victim that is substantially similar to a listed relationship, may also exercise these rights. The term "victim" does not include the accused or a person whom the court finds would not act in the best interests of a deceased, incompetent, minor, or incapacitated victim.

ARTICLE II: ELECTIVE FRANCHISE

Section 1. The general election of the state shall be held biennially as provided by law. Every citizen of the United States, who has attained the age of eighteen years and who is a North Dakota resident, shall be a qualified elector. When an elector moves within the state, he shall be entitled to vote in the precinct from which he moves until he establishes voting residence in another precinct. The legislative assembly shall provide by law for the determination of residence for voting eligibility, other than physical presence. No elector shall lose his residency for voting eligibility solely by reason of his absence from the state. The legislative assembly shall provide by law for secrecy in voting, for absentee voting, for administration of elections and for the nomination of candidates.

Section 2. No person who has been declared mentally incompetent by order of a court or other authority having jurisdiction, which order has not been rescinded, shall be qualified to vote. No person convicted of a felony shall be qualified to vote until his or her civil rights are restored.

ARTICLE III: POWERS RESERVED TO THE PEOPLE

Section 1. While the legislative power of this state shall be vested in a legislative assembly consisting of a senate and a house of representatives, the people reserve the power to propose and enact laws by the initiative, including the call for a constitutional convention; to approve or reject legislative Acts, or parts thereof, by the referendum; to propose and adopt constitutional amendments by the initiative; and to recall certain elected officials. This article is self-executing and all of its provisions are mandatory. Laws may be enacted to facilitate and safeguard, but not to hamper, restrict, or impair these powers.

Section 2. A petition to initiate or to refer a measure must be presented to the secretary of state for approval as to form. A request for approval must be presented over the names and signatures of twenty-five or more electors as sponsors, one of whom must be designated as chairman of the sponsoring committee. The secretary of state shall approve the petition for circulation if it is in proper form and contains the names and addresses of the sponsors and the full text of the measure. The legislative assembly may provide by law for a procedure through which the legislative council may establish an appropriate method for determining the fiscal impact of an initiative measure and for making the information regarding the fiscal impact of the measure available to the public.

Section 3. The petition shall be circulated only by electors. They shall swear thereon that the electors who have signed the petition did so in their presence. Each elector signing a petition shall also write in the date of signing and his post-office address. No law shall be enacted limiting the number of copies of a petition. The copies shall become part of the original petition when filed.

Section 4. The petition may be submitted to the secretary of state if signed by electors equal in number to two percent of the resident population of the state at the last federal decennial census.

Section 5. An initiative petition shall be submitted not less than one hundred twenty days before the statewide election at which the measure is to be voted upon. A referendum petition may be submitted only within ninety days after the filing of the measure with the secretary of state. The submission of a petition shall suspend the operation of any measure enacted by the legislative assembly except emergency measures and appropriation measures for the support and maintenance of state departments and institutions. The submission of a petition against one or more items or parts of any measure shall not prevent the remainder from going into effect. A referred measure may be voted upon at a statewide election or at a special election called by the governor.

Section 6. The secretary of state shall pass upon each petition, and if the secretary of state finds it insufficient, the secretary of state shall notify the "committee for the petitioners" and allow twenty days for correction. All decisions of the secretary of state in regard to any petition are subject to review by the supreme court. But if the sufficiency of the petition is being reviewed at the time the ballot is prepared, the secretary of state shall place the measure on the ballot and no subsequent decision shall invalidate the measure if it is at the election approved by a majority of the votes cast thereon. If proceedings are brought against any petition upon any ground, the burden of proof is upon the party attacking it and the proceedings must be filed with the supreme court no later than seventy-five days before the date of the statewide election at which the measure is to be voted upon.

Section 7. All decisions of the secretary of state in the petition process are subject to review by the supreme court in the exercise of original jurisdiction. A proceeding to review a decision of the secretary of state must be filed with the supreme court no later than seventy-five days before the date of the statewide election at which the measure is to be voted upon. If the decision of the secretary of state is being reviewed at the time the ballot is prepared, the secretary of state shall place the measure on the ballot and no court action shall invalidate the measure if it is approved at the election by a majority of the votes cast thereon.

Section 8. If a majority of votes cast upon an initiated or a referred measure are affirmative, it shall be deemed enacted. An initiated or referred measure which is approved shall become law thirty days after the election, and a referred measure which is rejected shall be void immediately. If conflicting measures are approved, the one receiving the highest number of affirmative votes shall be law. A measure approved by the electors may not be repealed or amended by the legislative assembly for seven years from its effective date, except by a two-thirds vote of the members elected to each house.

Section 9. A constitutional amendment may be proposed by initiative petition. If signed by electors equal in number to four percent of the resident population of the state at the last federal decennial census, the petition may be submitted to the secretary of state. All other provisions relating to initiative measures apply hereto.

Section 10. Any elected official of the state, of any county or of any legislative or county commissioner district shall be subject to recall by petition of electors equal in number to twenty-five percent of those who voted at the preceding general election for the office of governor in the state, county, or district in which the official is to be recalled. The petition shall be filed with the official with whom a petition for nomination to the office in question is filed, who shall call a special election if he finds the petition valid and sufficient. No elector may remove his name from a recall petition. The name of the official to be recalled shall be placed on the ballot unless he resigns within ten days after the filing of the petition. Other candidates for the office may be nominated in a manner provided by law. When the election results have been officially declared, the candidate receiving the highest number of votes shall be deemed elected for the remainder of the term. No official shall be subject twice to recall during the term for which he was elected.

ARTICLE IV: LEGISLATIVE BRANCH

Section 1. The senate must be composed of not less than forty nor more than fifty-four members, and the house of representatives must be composed of not less than eighty nor more than one hundred eight members. These houses are jointly designated as the legislative assembly of the state of North Dakota.

Section 2. The legislative assembly shall fix the number of senators and representatives and divide the state into as many senatorial districts of compact and contiguous territory as there are senators. The districts thus ascertained and determined after the 1990 federal decennial census shall continue until the adjournment of the first regular session after each federal decennial census, or until changed by law. The legislative assembly shall guarantee, as nearly as is practicable, that every elector is equal to every other elector in the state in the power to cast ballots for legislative candidates. A senator and at least two representatives must be apportioned to each senatorial district and be elected at large or from sub-districts from those districts. The legislative assembly may combine two senatorial districts only when a single member senatorial district includes a federal facility or federal installation, containing over two-thirds of the population of a single member senatorial district, and may provide for the election of senators at large and representatives at large or from sub-districts from those districts.

Section 3. The legislative assembly shall establish by law a procedure whereby one-half of the members of the senate and one-half of the members of the house of representatives, as nearly as is practicable, are elected biennially.

Section 4. Senators and representatives must be elected for terms of four years.

Section 5. Each individual elected or appointed to the legislative assembly must be, on the day of the election or appointment, a qualified elector in the district from which the member was selected and must have been a resident of the state for one year immediately prior to that election. An individual may not serve in the legislative assembly unless the individual lives in the district from which selected.

Section 6. While serving in the legislative assembly, no member may hold any full-time appointive state office established by this constitution or designated by law. During the term for which elected, no member of the legislative assembly may be appointed to any full-time office that has been created by the legislative assembly. During the term for which elected, no member of the legislative assembly may be appointed to any full-time office for which the legislative assembly has increased the compensation in an amount greater than the general rate of increase provided to full-time state employees.

Section 7. The terms of members of the legislative assembly begin on the first day of December following their election. The legislative assembly shall meet at the seat of government in the month of December following the election of the members thereof for organizational and orientation purposes as provided by law and shall thereafter recess until twelve noon on the first Tuesday after the third day in January or at such other time as may be prescribed by law but not later than the eleventh day of January. No regular session of the legislative assembly may exceed eighty natural days during the biennium. The organizational meeting of the legislative assembly may not be counted as part of those eighty natural days, nor may days spent in session at the call of the governor or while engaged in impeachment proceedings, be counted. Days spent in regular session need not be consecutive, and the legislative assembly may authorize its committees to meet at any time during the biennium. As used in this section, a "natural day" means a period of twenty-four consecutive hours. Neither house may recess nor adjourn for more than three days without consent of the other house.

Section 8. The house of representatives shall elect one of its members to act as presiding officer at the beginning of each organizational session.

Section 9. If any person elected to either house of the legislative assembly shall offer or promise to give his vote or influence, in favor of, or against any measure or proposition pending or proposed to be introduced into the legislative assembly, in consideration, or upon conditions, that any other person elected to the same legislative assembly will give, or will promise or assent to give, his vote or influence in favor of or against any other measure or proposition, pending or proposed to be introduced into such legislative assembly, the person making such offer or promise shall be deemed guilty of solicitation of bribery. If any member of the legislative assembly, shall give his vote or influence for or against any measure or proposition, pending or proposed to be introduced into such legislative assembly, or offer, promise or assent so to do upon condition that any other member will give, promise or assent to give his vote or influence in favor of or against any other such measure or proposition pending or proposed to be introduced into such legislative assembly, or in consideration that any other member hath given his vote or influence, for or against any other measure or proposition in such legislative assembly, he shall be deemed guilty of bribery. And any person, member of the legislative assembly or person elected thereto, who shall be guilty of either such offenses, shall be expelled, and shall not thereafter be eligible to the legislative assembly, and, on the conviction thereof in the civil courts, shall be liable to such further penalty as may be prescribed by law.

Section 10. No member of the legislative assembly, expelled for corruption, and no person convicted of bribery, perjury or other infamous crime shall be eligible to the legislative assembly, or to any office in either branch thereof.

Section 11. The legislative assembly may provide by law a procedure to fill vacancies occurring in either house of the legislative assembly.

Section 12. A majority of the members elected to each house constitutes a quorum. A smaller number may adjourn from day to day and may compel attendance of absent members in a manner, and under a penalty, as may be provided by law. Each house is the judge of the qualifications of its members, but election contests are subject to judicial review as provided by law. If two or more candidates for the same office receive an equal and highest number of votes, the secretary of state shall choose one of them by the toss of a coin. Each house shall determine its rules of procedure, and may punish its members or other persons for contempt or disorderly behavior in its presence. With the concurrence of two-thirds of its elected members, either house may expel a member.

Section 13. Each house shall keep a journal of its proceedings, and a recorded vote on any question shall be taken at the request of one-sixth of those members present. No bill may become law except by a recorded vote of a majority of the members elected to each house, and the lieutenant governor is considered a member-elect of the senate when the lieutenant governor votes. No law may be enacted except by a bill passed by both houses, and no bill may be amended on its passage through either house in a manner which changes its general subject matter. No bill may embrace more than one subject, which must be expressed in its title; but a law violating this provision is invalid only to the extent the subject is not so expressed. Every bill must be read on two separate natural days, and the readings may be by title only unless a reading at length is demanded by one-fifth of the members present. No bill may be amended, extended, or incorporated in any other bill by reference to its title only, except in the case of definitions and procedural provisions. The presiding officer of each house shall sign all bills passed and resolutions adopted by the legislative assembly, and the fact of signing shall be entered at once in the journal. Every law, except as otherwise provided in this section, enacted by the legislative assembly during its eighty natural meeting days takes effect on August first after its filing with the secretary of state, or if filed on or after August first and before January first of the following year ninety days after its filing, or on a subsequent date if specified in the law unless, by a vote of two-thirds of the members elected to each house, the legislative assembly declares it an emergency measure and includes the declaration in the Act. Every appropriation measure for support and maintenance of state departments and institutions and every tax measure that changes tax rates enacted by the legislative assembly take effect on July first after its filing with the secretary of state or on a subsequent date if specified in the law unless, by a vote of two-thirds of the members elected to each house, the legislative assembly declares it an emergency measure and includes the declaration in the Act. An emergency measure takes effect upon its filing with the secretary of state or on a date specified in the measure. Every law enacted by a special session of the legislative assembly takes effect on a date specified in the Act. The legislative assembly shall enact all laws necessary to carry into effect the provisions of this constitution. Except as otherwise provided in this constitution, no local or special laws may be enacted, nor may the legislative assembly indirectly enact special or local laws by the partial repeal of a general law but laws repealing local or special laws may be enacted.

Section 14. All sessions of the legislative assembly, including the committee of the whole and meetings of legislative committees, must be open and public.

Section 15. Members of the legislative assembly are immune from arrest during their attendance at the sessions, and in going to or returning from the sessions, except in cases of felony. Members of the legislative assembly may not be questioned in any other place for any words used in any speech or debate in legislative proceedings.

Section 16. Any amendment to this constitution may be proposed in either house of the legislative assembly, and if agreed to upon a roll call by a majority of the members elected to each house, must be submitted to the electors and if a majority of the votes cast thereon are in the affirmative, the amendment is a part of this constitution.

Sections 17. Repealed.

Section 18. Repealed.

Section 19. Renumbered.

Sections 20 to 46. Repealed.

ARTICLE V: EXECUTIVE BRANCH

Section 1. The executive power is vested in the governor, who shall reside in the state capital and shall hold the office for the term of four years beginning in the year 2000, and until a successor is elected and qualified.

Section 2. The qualified electors of the state at the times and places of choosing members of the legislative assembly shall choose a governor, lieutenant governor, agriculture commissioner, attorney general, auditor, insurance commissioner, three public service commissioners, secretary of state, superintendent of public instruction, tax commissioner, and treasurer. The legislative assembly may by law provide for a department of labor to be administered by a public official who may be either elected or appointed. The powers and duties of the agriculture commissioner, attorney general, auditor, insurance commissioner, public service commissioners, secretary of state, superintendent of public instruction, tax commissioner, and treasurer must be prescribed by law. If the legislative assembly establishes a labor department, the powers and duties of the officer administering that department must be prescribed by law.

Section 3. The governor and the lieutenant governor must be elected on a joint ballot. Each vote cast for a candidate for governor is deemed cast also for the candidate for lieutenant governor running jointly with the candidate for governor. The joint candidates having the highest number of votes must be declared elected. If two or more joint candidates have an equal and highest number of votes for governor and lieutenant governor, the legislative assembly in joint session at its next regular session shall choose one pair of joint candidates for the offices. The returns of the election for governor and lieutenant governor must be made in the manner prescribed by law.

Section 4. To be eligible to hold an elective office established by this article, a person must be a qualified elector of this state, must be at least twenty-five years of age on the day of the election, and must have been a resident of this state for the five years preceding election to office. To be eligible to hold the office of governor or lieutenant governor, a person must be at least thirty years old on the day of the election. The attorney general must be licensed to practice law in this state.

Section 5. The qualified electors shall choose the elected state officials at a time designated by the legislative assembly. The elected state officials shall serve until their successors are duly qualified. Terms of office of the elected officials except the public service commissioners are four years, except that in 2004 the agriculture commissioner, attorney general, secretary of state, and tax commissioner are elected to a term of two years. The terms of the public service commissioners are six years, so arranged that one of them is elected every two years. The terms of the governor and lieutenant governor begin on December fifteenth following their election. If two or more candidates for any executive office other than for governor and lieutenant governor receive an equal and highest number of votes, the legislative assembly in joint session shall choose one of them for the office.

Section 6. The elected state officials and the chief executive officers of the principal departments shall hold office in the state capital.

Section 7. The governor is the chief executive of the state. The governor shall have the responsibility to see that the state's business is well administered and that its laws are faithfully executed. The governor is commander-in-chief of the state's military forces, except when they are called into the service of the United States, and the governor may mobilize them to execute the laws and maintain order. The governor shall prescribe the duties of the lieutenant governor in addition to those prescribed in this article. The governor may call special sessions of the legislative assembly. The governor shall present information on the condition of the state, together with any recommended legislation, to every regular and special session of the legislative assembly. The governor shall transact and supervise all necessary business of the state with the United States, the other states, and the officers and officials of this state. The governor may grant reprieves, commutations, and pardons. The governor may delegate this power in a manner provided by law.

Section 8. The governor may fill a vacancy in any office by appointment if no other method is provided by this constitution or by law. If, while the senate is recessed or adjourned, a vacancy occurs in any office that is filled by appointment with senate confirmation, the governor shall make a temporary appointment to the office. When the senate reconvenes the governor shall make a nomination to fill the office. Except on request of the senate, no nominee rejected by the senate may again be nominated for that office at the same session, nor may the nominee be appointed to that office during a recess or adjournment of the senate.

Section 9. Every bill passed by the legislative assembly must be presented to the governor for the governor's signature. If the governor signs the bill, it becomes law. The governor may veto a bill passed by the legislative assembly. The governor may veto items in an appropriation bill. Portions of the bill not vetoed become law. The governor shall return for reconsideration any vetoed item or bill, with a written statement of the governor's objections, to the house in which it originated. That house shall immediately enter the governor's objections upon its journal. If, by a recorded vote, two-thirds of the members elected to that house pass a vetoed item or bill, it, along with the statement of the governor's objections, must immediately be delivered to the other house. If, by a recorded vote, two-thirds of the members elected to the other house also pass it, the vetoed item or bill becomes law. While the legislative assembly is in session, a bill becomes law if the governor neither signs nor vetoes it within three legislative days after its delivery to the governor. If the legislative assembly is not in session, a bill becomes law if the governor neither signs nor vetoes it within fifteen days, Saturdays and Sundays excepted, after its delivery to the governor.

Section 10. A governor who asks, receives, or agrees to receive any bribe upon any understanding that the governor's official opinion, judgment, or action shall be influenced thereby, or who gives or offers, or promises the governor's official influence in consideration that any member of the legislative assembly shall give the member's official vote or influence on any particular side of any question or matter upon which the member may be required to act in the member's official capacity, or who menaces any member by the threatened use of the governor's veto power, or who offers or promises any member that the governor will appoint any particular person or persons to any office created or thereafter to be created, in consideration that any member shall give the member's official vote or influence on any matter pending or thereafter to be introduced into either house of the legislative assembly, or who threatens any member that the governor will remove any person or persons from office or position with intent in any manner to influence the action of that member, must be punished in the manner now, or that may hereafter be, provided by law, and upon conviction thereof forfeits all right to hold or exercise any office of trust or honor in this state.

Section 11. The lieutenant governor shall succeed to the office of governor when a vacancy occurs in the office of governor. If, during a vacancy in the office of governor, the lieutenant governor is unable to serve because of death, impeachment, resignation, failure to qualify, removal from office, or disability, the secretary of state shall act as governor until the vacancy is filled or the disability removed.

Section 12. The lieutenant governor shall serve as president of the senate. If the senate is equally divided on a question, the lieutenant governor may vote on procedural matters and on substantive matters if the lieutenant governor's vote would be decisive.

ARTICLE VI: JUDICIAL BRANCH

Section 1. The judicial power of the state is vested in a unified judicial system consisting of a supreme court, a district court, and such other courts as may be provided by law.

Section 2. The supreme court shall be the highest court of the state. It shall have appellate jurisdiction, and shall also have original jurisdiction with authority to issue, hear, and determine such original and remedial writs as may be necessary to properly exercise its jurisdiction. The supreme court shall consist of five justices, one of whom shall be designated chief justice in the manner provided by law.

Section 3. The supreme court shall have authority to promulgate rules of procedure, including appellate procedure, to be followed by all the courts of this state; and, unless otherwise provided by law, to promulgate rules and regulations for the admission to practice, conduct, disciplining, and disbarment of attorneys at law. The chief justice shall be the administrative head of the unified judicial system. He may assign judges, including retired judges, for temporary duty in any court or district under such rules and regulations as may be promulgated by the supreme court. The chief justice shall appoint a court administrator for the unified judicial system. Unless otherwise provided by law, the powers, duties, qualifications, and terms of office of the court administrator, and other court officials, shall be as provided by rules of the court.

Section 4. A majority of the supreme court shall be necessary to constitute a quorum or to pronounce a decision, provided that the supreme court shall not declare a legislative enactment unconstitutional unless at least four of the members of the court so decide.

Section 5. When a judgment or order is reversed, modified, or confirmed by the supreme court, the reasons shall be concisely stated in writing, signed by the justices concurring, filed in the office of the clerk of the supreme court, and preserved with a record of the case. Any justice dissenting may give the reason for his dissent in writing over his signature.

Section 6. Appeals shall be allowed from decisions of lower courts to the supreme court as may be provided by law.

Section 7. The justices of the supreme court shall be chosen by the electors of the state for ten-year terms, so arranged that one justice is elected every two years. They shall hold office until their successors are duly qualified, and shall receive compensation as provided by law, but the compensation of any justice shall not be diminished during his term of office.

Section 8. The district court shall have original jurisdiction of all causes, except as otherwise provided by law, and such appellate jurisdiction as may be provided by law or by rule of the supreme court. The district court shall have authority to issue such writs as are necessary to the proper exercise of its jurisdiction.

Section 9. The state shall be divided into judicial districts by order of the supreme court. In each district, one or more judges, as provided by law, shall be chosen by the electors of the district. The term of office shall be six years, and a district judge shall hold office until his successor is duly qualified. The compensation of district judges shall be fixed by law, but the compensation of any district judge shall not be diminished during his term of office.

Section 10. Supreme court justices and district court judges shall be citizens of the United States and residents of this state, shall be learned in the law, and shall possess any additional qualifications prescribed by law. Judges of other courts shall be selected for such terms and shall have such qualifications as may be prescribed by law. No justice of the supreme court or judge of the district court of this state shall engage in the practice of law, or hold any public office, elective or appointive, not judicial in nature. No duties shall be imposed by law upon the supreme court or any of the justices thereof, except such as are judicial, nor shall any of the justices exercise any power of appointment except as herein provided. No judge of any court of this state shall be paid from the fees of his office, nor shall the amount of his compensation be measured by fees, other moneys received, or the amount of judicial activity of his office.

Section 11. When any justice or judge has a conflict of interest in a pending cause or is unable to sit in court because he is physically or mentally incapacitated, the chief justice, or a justice acting in his stead, shall assign a judge, or retired justice or judge, to hear the cause.

Section 12. The legislative assembly may provide for the retirement, discipline, and removal of judges. The removal procedure provided for herein may be used in addition to the impeachment proceedings provided for in article XI, sections 8, 9, and 10, and removal provided for in article XI, section 11.

Section 12.1. The legislative assembly may provide for the retirement, discipline and removal of judges of the supreme court and district court. The removal procedure provided for herein may be used in addition to the impeachment proceedings provided for in article XI, sections 8, 9, and 10.

Section 13.

1. A judicial nominating committee must be established by law. The governor shall fill any vacancy in the office of supreme court justice or district court judge by appointment from a list of candidates nominated by the committee, unless the governor calls a special election to fill the vacancy for the remainder of the term. Except as provided in subsection 2, an appointment must continue until the next general election, when the office must be filled by election for the remainder of the term.

2. An appointment must continue for at least two years. If the term of the appointed judgeship expires before the judge has served at least two years, the judge shall continue in the position until the next general election immediately following the service of at least two years.

3. Notwithstanding sections 7 and 9 of this article, the term of the judge elected at the subsequent general election provided for in subsection 2 is reduced to the number of years remaining in the subsequent term after the appointee has served at least two years.

ARTICLE VII: POLITICAL SUBDIVISIONS

Section 1. The purpose of this article is to provide for maximum local self-government by all political subdivisions with a minimum duplication of functions.

Section 2. The legislative assembly shall provide by law for the establishment and the government of all political subdivisions. Each political subdivision shall have and exercise such powers as provided by law.

Section 3. The several counties of the state of North Dakota as they now exist are hereby declared to be counties of the state of North Dakota.

Section 4. The legislative assembly shall provide by law for relocating county seats within counties, but it shall have no power to remove the county seat of any county.

Section 5. Methods and standards by which all or any portion of a county or counties may be annexed, merged, consolidated, reclassified, or dissolved shall be as provided by law. No portion of any county or counties shall be annexed, merged, consolidated, or dissolved unless a majority of the electors of each affected county voting on the question so approve.

Section 6. The legislative assembly shall provide by law for the establishment and exercise of home rule in counties and cities. No home rule charter shall become operative in any county or city until submitted to the electors thereof and approved by a majority of those voting thereon. In granting home rule powers to cities, the legislative assembly shall not be restricted by city debt limitations contained in this constitution.

Section 7. The legislative assembly shall also provide by law for optional forms of government for counties, but no optional form of government shall become operative in any county until submitted to the electors thereof at a special or general election, and approved by a majority of those voting thereon. Until one of the optional forms of county government is adopted by any county, the fiscal and administrative affairs of the county shall be governed by a board of county commissioners as provided by law.

Section 8. Each county shall provide for law enforcement, administrative and fiscal services, recording and registration services, educational services, and any other governmental services or functions as may be provided by law. Any elective office provided for by the counties shall be for a term of four years. Elective officers shall be elected by the electors in the jurisdiction in which the elected officer is to serve. A candidate for election for sheriff must be a resident in the jurisdiction in which the candidate is to serve at the time of the election. The office of sheriff shall be elected. The legislative assembly may provide by law for the election of any county elective officer, other than the sheriff, to serve one or more counties provided the affected counties agree to the arrangement and any candidate elected to the office is a qualified elector of one of the affected counties.

Section 9. Questions of the form of government to be adopted by any county or on the elimination or reinstatement of elective county offices may be placed upon the ballot by petition of electors of the county equal in number to twenty-five percent of the votes cast in the county for the office of governor at the preceding gubernatorial election.

Section 10. Agreements, including those for cooperative or joint administration of any powers or functions, may be made by any political subdivision with any other political subdivision, with the state, or with the United States, unless otherwise provided by law or home rule charter. A political subdivision may by mutual agreement transfer to the county in which it is located any of its powers or functions as provided by law or home rule charter, and may in like manner revoke the transfer.

Section 11. The power of the governing board of a city to franchise the construction and operation of any public utility or similar service within the city shall not be abridged by the legislative assembly.

ARTICLE VIII: EDUCATION

Section 1. A high degree of intelligence, patriotism, integrity and morality on the part of every voter in a government by the people being necessary in order to insure the continuance of that government and the prosperity and happiness of the people, the legislative assembly shall make provision for the establishment and maintenance of a system of public schools which shall be open to all children of the state of North Dakota and free from sectarian control. This legislative requirement shall be irrevocable without the consent of the United States and the people of North Dakota.

Section 2. The legislative assembly shall provide for a uniform system of free public schools throughout the state, beginning with the primary and extending through all grades up to and including schools of higher education, except that the legislative assembly may authorize tuition, fees and service charges to assist in the financing of public schools of higher education.

Section 3. In all schools instruction shall be given as far as practicable in those branches of knowledge that tend to impress upon the mind the vital importance of truthfulness, temperance, purity, public spirit, and respect for honest labor of every kind.

Section 4. The legislative assembly shall take such other steps as may be necessary to prevent illiteracy, secure a reasonable degree of uniformity in course of study, and to promote industrial, scientific, and agricultural improvements.

Section 5. All colleges, universities, and other educational institutions, for the support of which lands have been granted to this state, or which are supported by a public tax, shall remain under the absolute and exclusive control of the state. No money raised for the support of the public schools of the state shall be appropriated to or used for the support of any sectarian school.

Section 6. 1. A board of higher education, to be officially known as the state board of higher education, is hereby created for the control and administration of the following state educational institutions, to wit:

a. The state university and school of mines, at Grand Forks, with their substations.

b. The state agricultural college and experiment station, at Fargo, with their substations.

c. The school of science, at Wahpeton.

d. The state normal schools and teachers colleges, at Valley City, Mayville, Minot, and Dickinson.

e. The school of forestry, at Bottineau.

f. And such other state institutions of higher education as may hereafter be established.

2. a. The state board of higher education consists of eight members. The governor shall appoint seven members who are qualified electors and taxpayers of the state, and who have resided in this state for not less than five years immediately preceding their appointments. These seven appointments are subject to confirmation by the senate. The governor shall appoint as the eighth member of the board a full-time resident student in good academic standing at an institution under the jurisdiction of the state board. Except for the student member, no more than two persons holding a bachelor's degree from a particular institution under the jurisdiction of the state board of higher education may serve on the board at any one time. Except for the student member, no person employed by any institution under the control of the board shall serve as a member of the board and no employee of any such institution may be eligible for membership on the state board of higher education for a period of two years following the termination of employment.

The governor shall nominate from a list of three names for each position, selected by action of four of the following five persons: the president of the North Dakota education association, the chief justice of the supreme court, the superintendent of public instruction, the president pro tempore of the senate, and the speaker of the house of representatives and, with the consent of a majority of the members-elect of the senate, shall appoint from the list to the state board of higher education seven members. The governor shall ensure that the board membership is maintained in a balanced and representative manner. The term of office of members appointed to fill vacancies at the expiration of said terms shall be for four years, and in the case of vacancies otherwise arising, appointments shall be made only for the balance of the term of the members whose places are to be filled. A member may not be appointed to serve for more than two terms. If a member is appointed to fill a vacancy and serves two or more years of that term, the member is deemed to have served one full term.

b. In the event any nomination made by the governor is not consented to and confirmed by the senate, the governor shall again nominate a candidate selected from a new list. The nomination shall be submitted to the senate for confirmation and the proceedings shall continue until an appointee has been confirmed by the senate or the session of the legislature has adjourned.

c. If a term expires or a vacancy occurs when the legislature is not in session, the governor may appoint from a list selected as provided, a member who shall serve until the opening of the next session of the legislature, at which time the appointment must be certified to the senate for confirmation. If the appointee is not confirmed by the thirtieth legislative day of the session, the office shall be deemed vacant and the governor shall nominate another candidate for the office. The same proceedings shall be followed as are set forth in this section. If the legislature is in session at any time within six months prior to the date of the expiration of the term of any member, the governor shall nominate a successor from a list selected as above set forth, within the first thirty days of the session and upon confirmation by the senate the successor shall take office at the expiration of the incumbent's term. No person who has been nominated and whose nomination the senate has failed to confirm is eligible for an interim appointment. On or before July first of each year, beginning in 1995, the governor shall appoint a student member from a list of names recommended by the executive board of the North Dakota student association for a term of one year, beginning on July first. A student member may not serve more than two consecutive terms.

3. The members of the state board of higher education may only be removed by impeachment for the offenses and in the manner and according to the procedure provided for the removal of the governor by impeachment proceedings.

4. Each appointive member of the state board of higher education, except the student member, shall receive compensation set by the legislative assembly for the time actually spent devoted to the duties of the member's office. All members shall receive necessary expenses in the same manner and amounts as other state officials for attending meetings and performing other functions of their office.

5. The legislature shall provide adequate funds for the proper carrying out of the functions and duties of the state board of higher education.

6. a. The state board of higher education shall hold its first meeting at the office of the state board of administration at Bismarck, on the 6th day of July, 1939, and shall organize and elect one of its members as president of such board for a term of one year. It shall also at said meeting, or as soon thereafter as may be practicable, elect a competent person as secretary, who shall reside during his term of office in the city of Bismarck, North Dakota. Said secretary shall hold office at the will of the board. As soon as said board is established and organized, it shall assume all the powers and perform all the duties now conferred by law upon the board of administration in connection with the several institutions hereinbefore mentioned, and the said board of administration shall immediately upon the organization of said state board of higher education, surrender and transfer to said state board of higher education all duties, rights, and powers granted to it under the existing laws of this state concerning the institutions hereinbefore mentioned, together with all property, deeds, records, reports, and appurtenances of every kind belonging or appertaining to said institutions.

b. The said state board of higher education shall have full authority over the institutions under its control with the right, among its other powers, to prescribe, limit, or modify the courses offered at the several institutions. In furtherance of its powers, the state board of higher education shall have the power to delegate to its employees details of the administration of the institutions under its control. The said state board of higher education shall have full authority to organize or reorganize within constitutional and statutory limitations, the work of each institution under its control, and do each and everything necessary and proper for the efficient and economic administration of said state educational institutions.

c. Said board shall prescribe for all of said institutions standard systems of accounts and records and shall biennially, and within six (6) months immediately preceding the regular session of the legislature, make a report to the governor, covering in detail the operations of the educational institutions under its control.

d. It shall be the duty of the heads of the several state institutions hereinbefore mentioned, to submit the budget requests for the biennial appropriations for said institutions to said state board of higher education; and said state board of higher education shall consider said budgets and shall revise the same as in its judgment shall be for the best interests of the educational system of the state; and thereafter the state board of higher education shall prepare and present to the state budget board and to the legislature a single unified budget covering the needs of all the institutions under its control. "Said budget shall be prepared and presented by the board of administration until the state board of higher education organizes as provided in subsection 6a." The appropriations for all of said institutions shall be contained in one legislative measure. The budgets and appropriation measures for the agricultural experiment stations and their substations and the extension division of the North Dakota state university of agriculture and applied science may be separate from those of state educational institutions.

e. The said state board of higher education shall have the control of the expenditure of the funds belonging to, and allocated to such institutions and also those appropriated by the legislature, for the institutions of higher education in this state; provided, however, that funds appropriated by the legislature and specifically designated for any one or more of such institutions, shall not be used for any other institution.

7. a. The state board of higher education shall, as soon as practicable, appoint for a term of not to exceed three (3) years, a state commissioner of higher education, whose principal office shall be at the state capitol, in the city of Bismarck. Said commissioner of higher education shall be responsible to the state board of higher education and shall be removable by said board for cause.

b. The state commissioner of higher education shall be a graduate of some reputable college or university, and who by training and experience is familiar with the problems peculiar to higher education.

c. Such commissioner of higher education shall be the chief executive officer of said state board of higher education, and shall perform such duties as shall be prescribed by the board.

8. This constitutional provision shall be self-executing and shall become effective without the necessity of legislative action.

ARTICLE IX: TRUST LANDS

Section 1. All proceeds of the public lands that have been, or may be granted by the United States for the support of the common schools in this state; all such per centum as may be granted by the United States on the sale of public lands; the proceeds of property that fall to the state by escheat; all gifts, donations, or the proceeds thereof that come to the state for support of the common schools, or not otherwise appropriated by the terms of the gift, and all other property otherwise acquired for common schools, must be and remain a perpetual trust fund for the maintenance of the common schools of the state. All property, real or personal, received by the state from whatever source, for any specific educational or charitable institution, unless otherwise designated by the donor, must be and remain a perpetual trust fund for the creation and maintenance of such institution, and may be commingled only with similar funds for the same institution. If a gift is made to an institution for a specific purpose, without designating a trustee, the gift may be placed in the institution's fund; provided that such a donation may be expended as the terms of the gift provide. Revenues earned by a perpetual trust fund must be deposited in the fund. The costs of administering a perpetual trust fund may be paid out of the fund. The perpetual trust funds must be managed to preserve their purchasing power and to maintain stable distributions to fund beneficiaries.

Section 2. Distributions from the common schools trust fund, together with the net proceeds of all fines for violation of state laws and all other sums which may be added by law, must be faithfully used and applied each year for the benefit of the common schools of the state and no part of the fund must ever be diverted, even temporarily, from this purpose or used for any purpose other than the maintenance of common schools as provided by law. Distributions from an educational or charitable institution's trust fund must be faithfully used and applied each year for the benefit of the institution and no part of the fund may ever be diverted, even temporarily, from this purpose or used for any purpose other than the maintenance of the institution, as provided by law. For the biennium during which this amendment takes effect, distributions from the perpetual trust funds must be the greater of the amount distributed in the preceding biennium or ten percent of the five-year average value of trust assets, excluding the value of lands and minerals. Thereafter, biennial distributions from the perpetual trust funds must be ten percent of the five-year average value of trust assets, excluding the value of lands and minerals. The average value of trust assets is determined by using the assets' ending value for the fiscal year that ends one year before the beginning of the biennium and the assets' ending value for the four preceding fiscal years. Equal amounts must be distributed during each year of the biennium.

Section 3. The superintendent of public instruction, governor, attorney general, secretary of state and state treasurer comprise a board of commissioners, to be denominated the "board of university and school lands". Subject to the provisions of this article and any law that may be passed by the legislative assembly, the board has control of the appraisement, sale, rental, and disposal of all school and university lands, and the proceeds from the sale of such lands shall be invested as provided by law.

Section 4. The public officers designated by law shall constitute boards of appraisal and under the authority of the state board of university and school lands shall appraise all school lands within their respective counties which they may from time to time recommend for sale at their actual value under the prescribed terms and shall first select and designate for sale the most valuable lands.

Section 5. After one year from the assembling of the first legislative assembly the lands granted to the state from the United States for the support of the common schools, may be sold upon the following conditions and no other: No more than one-fourth of all such lands shall be sold within the first five years after the same become salable by virtue of this section. No more than one-half of the remainder within ten years after the same become salable as aforesaid. The residue may be sold at any time after the expiration of said ten years. The legislative assembly shall provide for the sale of all school lands subject to the provisions of this article. In all sales of lands subject to the provisions of this article all minerals therein, including but not limited to oil, gas, coal, cement materials, sodium sulfate, sand and gravel, road material, building stone, chemical substances, metallic ores, uranium ores, or colloidal or other clays, shall be reserved and excepted to the state of North Dakota, except that leases may be executed for the extraction and sale of such materials in such manner and upon such terms as the legislative assembly may provide.

Section 6. No original grant school or institutional land shall be sold for less than the fair market value thereof, and in no case for less than ten dollars ($10.00) per acre, provided that when lands have been sold on contract and the contract has been canceled, such lands may be resold without re-appraisement by the board of appraisal. The purchaser shall pay twenty (20) percent of the purchase price at the time the contract is executed; thereafter annual payments shall be made of not less than six (6) percent of the original purchase price. An amount equal to not less than three (3) percent per annum of the unpaid principal shall be credited to interest and the balance shall be applied as payment on principal as credit on purchase price. The purchaser may pay all or any installment or installments not yet due to any interest paying date. If the purchaser so desires, he may pay the entire balance due on his contract with interest to date of payment at any time and he will then be entitled to proper conveyance. All sales shall be held at the county seat of the county in which the land to be sold is situated, and shall be at public auction and to the highest bidder, and notice of such sale shall be published once each week for a period of three weeks prior to the day of sale in a legal newspaper published nearest the land and in the newspaper designated for the publication of the official proceedings and legal notices within the county in which said land is situated. No grant or patent for such lands shall issue until payment is made for the same; provided that the land contracted to be sold by the state shall be subject to taxation from the date of the contract. In case the taxes assessed against any of said lands for any year remain unpaid until the first Monday in October of the following year, the contract of sale for such land shall, if the board of university and school lands so determine, by it, be declared null and void. No contract of sale heretofore made under the provisions of this section of the constitution as then providing shall be affected by this amendment, except prepayment of principal may be made as herein provided. Any of said lands that may be required for townsite purposes, schoolhouse sites, church sites, cemetery sites, sites for other educational or charitable institutions, public parks, airplane landing fields, fairgrounds, public highways, railroad right of way, or other railroad uses and purposes, reservoirs for the storage of water for irrigation, irrigation canals, and ditches, drainage ditches, or for any of the purposes for which private lands may be taken under the right of eminent domain under the constitution and laws of this state, may be sold under the provisions of this article, and shall be paid for in full at the time of sale, or at any time thereafter as herein provided. Any of said lands and any other lands controlled by the board of university and school lands, including state coal mineral interests, may, with the approval of said board, be exchanged for lands and coal mineral interests of the United States, the state of North Dakota or any county or municipality thereof as the legislature may provide, and the lands so acquired shall be subject to the trust to which the lands exchanged therefor were subject, and the state shall reserve all mineral and water power rights in land so transferred, except coal mineral interests approved for exchange by the board of university and school lands under this section. When any of said lands have been heretofore or may be hereafter sold on contract, and the purchaser or his heirs or assigns is unable to pay in full for the land purchased within twenty years after the date of purchase and such contract is in default and subject to being declared null and void as by law provided, the board of university and school lands may, after declaring such contract null and void, resell the land described in such contract to such purchaser, his heirs or assigns, for the amount of the unpaid principal, together with interest thereon reckoned to the date of such resale at the rate of not less than three (3%) percent, but in no case shall the resale price be more than the original sale price; such contract of resale shall be upon the terms herein provided, provided this section shall be deemed self-executing insofar as the provisions for resale herein made are concerned.

Section 7. All lands received by the state for any specific educational or charitable institution shall be appraised and sold in the same manner and under the same limitations and subject to all the conditions as to price and sale as provided in this constitution for the appraisal and sale of lands for the benefit of common schools. However, a distinct and separate account shall be kept by the proper officers of each of said funds and the limitations as to the time in which school land may be sold shall apply only to lands granted for the support of common schools.

Section 8. The legislative assembly shall have authority to provide by law for the leasing of lands granted to the state for educational and charitable purposes; but no such law shall authorize the leasing of said lands for a longer period than five years. Said lands shall only be leased for pasturage and meadow purposes and at a public auction after notice as heretofore provided in case of sale; provided, that all of said school lands now under cultivation may be leased, at the discretion and under the control of the board of university and school lands, for other than pasturage and meadow purposes until sold. All rents shall be paid in advance. Provided, further, that coal lands may also be leased for agricultural cultivation upon such terms and conditions and for such a period, not exceeding five years, as the legislature may provide.

Section 9. No law shall ever be passed by the legislative assembly granting to any person, corporation or association any privileges by reason of the occupation, cultivation or improvement of any public lands by said person, corporation or association subsequent to the survey thereof by the general government. No claim for the occupation, cultivation or improvement of any public lands shall ever be recognized, nor shall such occupation, cultivation or improvement of any public lands ever be used to diminish either directly or indirectly, the purchase price of said lands.

Section 10. The legislative assembly may provide by law for the sale or disposal of all public lands that have been, or may hereafter be granted by the United States to the state for purposes other than set forth in article IX, section 1. The legislative assembly in providing for the appraisal, sale, rental, and disposal of the same shall not be subject to the provisions and limitations of article IX, sections 1 through 11.

Section 11. The legislative assembly shall pass suitable laws for the safekeeping, transfer and disbursement of the state school funds; and shall require all officers charged with the same or the safekeeping thereof to give ample bonds for all moneys and funds received by them, and if any of said officers shall convert to his own use in any manner or form, or shall loan with or without interest or shall deposit in his own name, or otherwise than in the name of the state of North Dakota, or shall deposit in any banks or with any person or persons, or exchange for other funds or property any portion of the school funds aforesaid or purposely allow any portion of the same to remain in his own hands uninvested, except in the manner prescribed by law, every such act shall constitute an embezzlement of so much of the aforesaid school funds as shall be thus taken or loaned, or deposited, or exchanged, or withheld and shall be a felony; and any failure to pay over, produce or account for, the state school funds or any part of the same entrusted to any such officer, as by law required or demanded, shall be held and be taken to be prima facie evidence of such embezzlement.

Section 12. The following public institutions of the state are permanently located at the places hereinafter named, each to have the lands specifically granted to it by the United States in the Act of Congress approved February 22, 1889, to be disposed of and used in such manner as the legislative assembly may prescribe subject to the limitations provided in the article on school and public lands contained in this constitution.

1. The seat of government at the city of Bismarck in the county of Burleigh.

2. The state university and the school of mines at the city of Grand Forks, in the county of Grand Forks.

3. The North Dakota state university of agriculture and applied science at the city of Fargo, in the county of Cass.

4. A state normal school at the city of Valley City, in the county of Barnes, and the legislative assembly, in apportioning the grant of eighty thousand acres of land for normal schools made in the Act of Congress referred to shall grant to the said normal school at Valley City, as aforementioned, fifty thousand (50,000) acres, and said lands are hereby appropriated to said institution for that purpose.

5. The school for the deaf and dumb of North Dakota at the city of Devils Lake, in the county of Ramsey.

6. A state training school at the city of Mandan, in the county of Morton.

7. A state normal school at the city of Mayville, in the county of Traill, and the legislative assembly in apportioning the grant of lands made by Congress in the Act aforesaid for state normal schools shall assign thirty thousand (30,000) acres to the institution hereby located at Mayville, and said lands are hereby appropriated for said purpose.

8. A state hospital for the insane at the city of Jamestown, in the county of Stutsman. And the legislative assembly shall appropriate twenty thousand acres of the grant of lands made by the Act of Congress aforesaid for other educational and charitable institutions to the benefit and for the endowment of said institution, and there shall be located at or near the city of Grafton, in the county of Walsh, an institution for the feeble-minded, on the grounds purchased by the secretary of the interior for a penitentiary building.

Section 13. The following public institutions are located as provided, each to have so much of the remaining grant of one hundred seventy thousand acres of land made by the United States for "other educational and charitable institutions" as is allotted by law:

1. A soldiers' home, when located, or such other charitable institution as the legislative assembly may determine, at the city of Lisbon in the county of Ransom, with a grant of forty thousand acres of land.

2. The school for the blind at the city of Grand Forks in the county of Grand Forks or at such other location as may be determined by the legislative assembly to be in the best interests of the students of such institution and the state of North Dakota.

3. A school of forestry, or such other institution as the legislative assembly may determine, at such place in one of the counties of McHenry, Ward, Bottineau, or Rolette, as the electors of said counties may determine by an election for that purpose, to be held as provided by the legislative assembly.

4. A school of science or such other educational or charitable institution as the legislative assembly may prescribe, at the city of Wahpeton in the county of Richland, with a grant of forty thousand acres.

5. A state college at the city of Minot in the county of Ward.

6. A state college at the city of Dickinson in the county of Stark.

7. A state hospital for the mentally ill at such place within this state as shall be selected by the legislative assembly. No other institution of a character similar to any one of those located by article IX, section 12, or this section shall be established or maintained without an amendment of this constitution.

ARTICLE X: FINANCE AND PUBLIC DEBT

Section 1. The legislative assembly shall be prohibited from raising revenue to defray the expenses of the state through the levying of a tax on the assessed value of real or personal property.

Section 2. The power of taxation shall never be surrendered or suspended by any grant or contract to which the state or any county or other municipal corporation shall be a party.

Section 3. No tax shall be levied except in pursuance of law, and every law imposing a tax shall state distinctly the object of the same, to which only it shall be applied. Notwithstanding the foregoing or any other provisions of this constitution, the legislative assembly, in any law imposing a tax or taxes on, in respect to or measured by income, may define the income on, in respect to or by which such tax or taxes are imposed or measured or may define the tax itself by reference to any provision of the laws of the United States as the same may be or become effective at any time or from time to time, and may prescribe exceptions or modifications to any such provision.

Section 4. All taxable property except as hereinafter in this section provided, shall be assessed in the county, city, township, village or district in which it is situated, in the manner prescribed by law. The property, including franchises of all railroads operated in this state, and of all express companies, freight line companies, dining car companies, sleeping car companies, car equipment companies, or private car line companies, telegraph or telephone companies, the property of any person, firm or corporation used for the purpose of furnishing electric light, heat or power, or in distributing the same for public use, and the property of any other corporation, firm or individual now or hereafter operating in this state, and used directly or indirectly in the carrying of persons, property or messages, shall be assessed by the state board of equalization in a manner prescribed by such state board or commission as may be provided by law. But should any railroad allow any portion of its railway to be used for any purpose other than the operation of a railroad thereon, such portion of its railway, while so used shall be assessed in a manner provided for the assessment of other real property.

Section 5. Taxes shall be uniform upon the same class of property including franchises within the territorial limits of the authority levying the tax. The legislative assembly may by law exempt any or all classes of personal property from taxation and within the meaning of this section, fixtures, buildings and improvements of every character, whatsoever, upon land shall be deemed personal property. The property of the United States, to the extent immunity from taxation has not been waived by an act of Congress, property of the state, county, and municipal corporations, to the extent immunity from taxation has not been waived by an act of the legislative assembly, and property used exclusively for schools, religious, cemetery, charitable or other public purposes shall be exempt from taxation. Real property used for conservation or wildlife purposes is not exempt from taxation unless an exemption is provided by the legislative assembly. Except as restricted by this article, the legislative assembly may provide for raising revenue and fixing the situs of all property for the purpose of taxation. Provided that all taxes and exemptions in force when this amendment is adopted shall remain in force until otherwise provided by statute.

Section 6. Repealed.

Section 7. The legislature may by law provide for the levy and collection of an acreage tax on lands within the state in addition to the limitations specified in article X, section 1, of the constitution. The proceeds of such tax shall be used to indemnify the owners of growing crops against damages by hail, provided that lands used exclusively for public roads, rights of way of common carriers, mining, manufacturing or pasturage may be exempt from such tax.

Section 8. The legislative assembly shall pass all laws necessary to carry out the provisions of this article.

Section 9. The legislative assembly may provide for the levy of a tax upon lands within the state for the purpose of creating a fund to insure the owners of growing crops against losses by hail. The legislative assembly may classify lands within the state, and divide the state into districts on such basis as shall seem just and necessary, and may vary the tax rates in such districts in accordance with the risk, in order to secure an equitable distribution of the burden of the tax among the owners of such lands. Section

10. 1. Upon the adoption of this amendment to the Constitution of the State of North Dakota there shall be annually levied by the state of North Dakota one mill upon all of the taxable property within the state of North Dakota which, when collected, shall be covered into the state treasury of the state of North Dakota and placed to the credit of the North Dakota state medical center at the university of North Dakota; said fund shall be expended as the legislature shall direct for the development and maintenance necessary to the efficient operation of the said North Dakota state medical center.

2. This amendment shall be self-executing, but legislation may be enacted to facilitate its operation. Section 11. Revenue from gasoline and other motor fuel excise and license taxation, motor vehicle registration and license taxes, except revenue from aviation gasoline and unclaimed aviation motor fuel refunds and other aviation motor fuel excise and license taxation used by aircraft, after deduction of cost of administration and collection authorized by legislative appropriation only, and statutory refunds, shall be appropriated and used solely for construction, reconstruction, repair and maintenance of public highways, and the payment of obligations incurred in the construction, reconstruction, repair and maintenance of public highways.

Section 12. 1. All public moneys, from whatever source derived, shall be paid over monthly by the public official, employee, agent, director, manager, board, bureau, or institution of the state receiving the same, to the state treasurer, and deposited by him to the credit of the state, and shall be paid out and disbursed only pursuant to appropriation first made by the legislature; provided, however, that there is hereby appropriated the necessary funds required in the financial transactions of the Bank of North Dakota, and required for the payment of losses, duly approved, payable from the state hail insurance fund, state bonding fund, and state fire and tornado fund, and required for the payment of compensation to injured employees or death claims, duly approved, payable from the workmen's compensation fund, and required for authorized investments made by the board of university and school lands, and required for the financial operations of the state mill and elevator association, and required for the payment of interest and principal of bonds and other fixed obligations of the state, and required for payments required by law to be paid to beneficiaries of the teachers' insurance and retirement fund, and required for refunds made under the provisions of the Retail Sales Tax Act, and the State Income Tax Law, and the State Gasoline Tax Law, and the Estate and Succession Tax Law, and the income of any state institution derived from permanent trust funds, and the funds allocated under the law to the state highway department and the various counties for the construction, reconstruction, and maintenance of public roads. This constitutional amendment shall not be construed to apply to fees and moneys received in connection with the licensing and organization of physicians and surgeons, pharmacists, dentists, osteopaths, optometrists, embalmers, barbers, lawyers, veterinarians, nurses, chiropractors, accountants, architects, hairdressers, chiropodists, and other similarly organized, licensed trades and professions; and this constitutional amendment shall not be construed to amend or repeal existing laws or Acts amendatory thereof concerning such fees and moneys.

2. No bills, claims, accounts, or demands against the state or any county or other political subdivision shall be audited, allowed, or paid until a full itemized statement in writing shall be filed with the officer or officers whose duty it may be to audit the same, and then only upon warrant drawn upon the treasurer of such funds by the proper officer or officers.

3. This amendment shall become effective on July 1, 1939.

Section 13. The state may issue or guarantee the payment of bonds, provided that all bonds in excess of two million dollars shall be secured by first mortgage upon real estate in amounts not to exceed sixty-five percent of its value; or upon real and personal property of state-owned utilities, enterprises, or industries, in amounts not exceeding its value, and provided further, that the state shall not issue or guarantee bonds upon property of state-owned utilities, enterprises, or industries in excess of ten million dollars. No further indebtedness shall be incurred by the state unless evidenced by a bond issue, which shall be authorized by law for certain purposes, to be clearly defined. Every law authorizing a bond issue shall provide for levying an annual tax, or make other provision, sufficient to pay the interest semiannually, and the principal within thirty years from the date of the issue of such bonds and shall specially appropriate the proceeds of such tax, or of such other provisions to the payment of said principal and interest, and such appropriation shall not be repealed nor the tax or other provisions discontinued until such debt, both principal and interest, shall have been paid. No debt in excess of the limit named herein shall be incurred except for the purpose of repelling invasion, suppressing insurrection, defending the state in time of war or to provide for the public defense in case of threatened hostilities.

Section 14. 1. Notwithstanding any other provision in the constitution, and for the purpose of promoting the economic growth of the state, the development of its natural resources, and the prosperity and welfare of its people, the state may issue bonds and use the proceeds thereof to make loans to privately or cooperatively owned enterprises to plan, construct, acquire, equip, improve, and extend facilities for converting natural resources into power and generating and transmitting such power, and to acquire real and personal property and water and mineral rights needed for such facilities.

2. The state may issue general obligation bonds for this purpose to an amount which, with all outstanding general obligation bonds, less the amount of all money on hand and taxes in process of collection which are appropriated for their payment, will not exceed five percent of the full and true value of all of the taxable property in the state, to be ascertained by the last assessment made for state and county purposes: but nothing herein shall increase or diminish the limitations established by other provisions of the constitution on the amount of bonds therein authorized to be issued.

3. The state may also issue revenue bonds for the purpose of providing part or all of the funds required for any project undertaken under subsection 1, payable solely from sums realized from payments of principal and interest on money loaned for such project, and from other similar projects if so determined by the legislature, and from the liquidation of security given for such payments. Revenue bonds issued for any project shall not exceed the cost thereof, including all expenses reasonably incurred to complete and finance the project, but shall not be subject to any other limitation of amount.

4. The full faith and credit of the state shall be pledged for the prompt and full payment of all bonds issued under subsection 2. Its obligation with respect to bonds issued under subsection 3 shall be limited to the prompt and full performance of such covenants as the legislature may authorize to be made respecting the enforcing of the provisions of underlying loan agreements and the segregation, accounting, and application of bond proceeds and of loan payments and other security pledged for the payment of the bonds. All bonds authorized by subsections 1 to 3, inclusive, shall mature within forty years from their respective dates of issue, but may be refunded at or before maturity in such manner and for such term and upon such conditions as the legislature may direct. Any such bonds may, but need not be, secured by mortgage upon real or personal property acquired with the proceeds of the same or any other issue of general obligation or revenue bonds, or upon other property mortgaged by the debtor. Pledges of revenues and mortgages of property securing bonds of any issue may be prior or subordinate to or on a parity with pledges and mortgages securing any other issue of general obligation or revenue bonds, as determined by the legislature from time to time in conformity with any provisions made for the security of outstanding bonds.

5. The legislature shall pass such laws as are appropriate to implement this amendment.

6. If any subsection of this amendment, or any part of a subsection, or any application thereof to particular circumstances should be held invalid for any reason, such invalidity shall not affect the validity of all remaining provisions of this amendment which may be given effect without that which is declared invalid, as applied to any circumstances and for this purpose all subsections and parts of subsections and applications thereof are declared to be severable.

Section 15. The debt of any county, township, city, town, school district or any other political subdivision, shall never exceed five per centum upon the assessed value of the taxable property therein; provided that any incorporated city may, by a two-thirds vote, increase such indebtedness three per centum on such assessed value beyond said five per centum limit, and a school district, by a majority vote may increase such indebtedness five percent on such assessed value beyond said five per centum limit; provided also that any county or city by a majority vote may issue bonds upon any revenue-producing utility owned by such county or city, or for the purchasing or acquiring the same or building or establishment thereof, in amounts not exceeding

the physical value of such utility, industry or enterprise. In estimating the indebtedness which a city, county, township, school district or any other political subdivision may incur, the entire amount, exclusive of the bonds upon said revenue-producing utilities, whether contracted prior or subsequent to the adoption of this constitution, shall be included; provided further that any incorporated city may become indebted in any amount not exceeding four per centum of such assessed value without regard to the existing indebtedness of such city for the purpose of constructing or purchasing waterworks for furnishing a supply of water to the inhabitants of such city, or for the purpose of constructing sewers, and for no other purposes whatever. All bonds and obligations in excess of the amount of indebtedness permitted by this constitution, given by any city, county, township, town, school district, or any other political subdivision shall be void.
4

Section 16. Any city, county, township, town, school district or any other political subdivision incurring indebtedness shall, at or before the time of so doing, provide for the collection of an annual tax sufficient to pay the interest and also the principal thereof when due, and all laws or ordinances providing for the payment of the interest or principal of any debt shall be irrepealable until such debt be paid.

Section 17. No bond or evidence of indebtedness of the state is valid unless it has endorsed thereon a certificate, signed by the auditor and secretary of state showing that the bond or evidence of debt is issued pursuant to law and is within the debt limit. No bond or evidence of debt of any county, or bond of any township or other political subdivision is valid unless it has endorsed thereon a certificate signed by the officer authorized by law to sign such certificate, stating that said bond or evidence of debt is issued pursuant to law and is within the debt limit.

Section 18. The state, any county or city may make internal improvements and may engage in any industry, enterprise or business, not prohibited by article XX of the constitution, but neither the state nor any political subdivision thereof shall otherwise loan or give its credit or make donations to or in aid of any individual, association or corporation except for reasonable support of the poor, nor subscribe to or become the owner of capital stock in any association or corporation.

Section 19. The legislative assembly is hereby authorized and empowered to provide by law for the erection, purchasing or leasing and operation of one or more terminal grain elevators in the states of Minnesota or Wisconsin, or both, to be maintained and operated in such manner as the legislative assembly shall prescribe, and provide for inspection, weighing and grading of all grain received in such elevator or elevators.

Section 20. The legislative assembly is hereby authorized and empowered to provide by law for the erection, purchasing or leasing and operation of one or more terminal grain elevators in the state of North Dakota, to be maintained and operated in such manner as the legislative assembly shall prescribe, and provide for inspection, weighing and grading of all grain received in such elevator or elevators.

Section 21. Not less than fifteen percent of the tax imposed for severing coal shall be placed into a permanent trust fund in the state treasury to be held in trust and administered by the board of university and school lands, which shall have full authority to invest said trust funds as provided by law, and may loan moneys from the fund to political subdivisions as provided by law. The interest earned on the moneys in said trust fund shall be used first to replace uncollectable loans made from the fund, and the balance shall be credited to the general fund of the state. Up to fifty percent of the taxes collected and deposited in the permanent trust fund during a biennium may be appropriated by the legislative assembly for lignite research, development, and marketing as provided by law. An additional twenty percent of the taxes collected and deposited in the permanent trust fund during a biennium may be appropriated by the legislative assembly for clean coal demonstration projects approved by the industrial commission.

Section 22. The legislative assembly may provide by law for a percentage of revenue from taxes imposed on the extraction or production of oil to be allocated and credited to a special trust fund, to be known as the resources trust fund. The principal and income of the resources trust fund may be expended only pursuant to legislative appropriation for: 1. Constructing water-related projects, including rural water systems; and 2. Funding of programs for energy conservation.

Section 23. The legislative assembly may provide for the payment of adjusted compensation to North Dakota residents who were members of the regular active duty armed forces and who served in the Persian Gulf theatre or in the Grenada, Lebanon, or Panama areas of armed conflict as designated by the President of the United States or to heirs of North Dakota residents who were members of the regular active duty armed forces and who died while on orders to or from the Persian Gulf theatre or in the Grenada, Lebanon, or Panama areas of armed conflict as designated by the President of the United States. The legislative assembly may provide a direct appropriation or provide for the issuance, sale, and delivery of bonds of the state of North Dakota in such principal amounts as determined by the legislative assembly to be necessary for the payment of adjusted compensation under this section. Adjusted compensation under this section may be paid at such rates, terms of service, and conditions as the legislative assembly provides.

Section 24. 1. Ten percent of the revenue from oil extraction taxes from taxable oil produced in this state must be deposited in the common schools trust fund.

2. Ten percent of the revenue from oil extraction taxes from taxable oil produced in this state must be deposited in the foundation aid stabilization fund in the state treasury, the interest of which must be transferred to the state general fund on July first of each year.

a. Except as otherwise provided, the principal of the foundation aid stabilization fund may be expended upon order of the governor, who may direct such a transfer only to offset reductions in state aid to school districts, which were made by executive action pursuant to law, due to a revenue shortage.

b. Whenever the principal balance of the foundation aid stabilization fund exceeds fifteen percent of the general fund appropriation for state aid to school districts, for the most recently completed biennium, as determined by the office of management and budget, the legislative assembly may appropriate or transfer any excess principal balance. Such amount may be used for education-related purposes, as provided by law.

Section 25. The veterans' postwar trust fund shall be a permanent trust fund of the state of North Dakota and shall consist of moneys transferred or credited to the fund as authorized by legislative enactment. Investment of the fund shall be the responsibility of the state treasurer who shall have full authority to invest the fund only in the same manner as the state investment board is authorized to make investments. All income received from investments is to be utilized for programs which must be of benefit and service to veterans, who are defined by legislative enactment, or their dependents, and such income is hereby appropriated to the administrative committee on veterans' affairs on a continuing basis for expenditure upon those programs selected at the discretion of the administrative committee on veterans' affairs.

Section 26. 1. Thirty percent of total revenue derived from taxes on oil and gas production or extraction must be transferred by the state treasurer to a special fund in the state treasury known as the legacy fund. The legislative assembly may transfer funds from any source into the legacy fund and such transfers become part of the principal of the legacy fund.

2. The principal and earnings of the legacy fund may not be expended until after June 30, 2017, and an expenditure of principal after that date requires a vote of at least two-thirds of the members elected to each house of the legislative assembly. Not more than fifteen percent of the principal of the legacy fund may be expended during a biennium.

3. Statutory programs, in existence as a result of legislation enacted through 2009, providing for impact grants, direct revenue allocations to political subdivisions, and deposits in the oil and gas research fund must remain in effect but the legislative assembly may adjust statutory allocations for those purposes. The state investment board shall invest the principal of the North Dakota legacy fund. The state treasurer shall transfer earnings of the North Dakota legacy fund accruing after June 30, 2017, to the state general fund at the end of each biennium.

Section 27. The state and any county, township, city, or any other political subdivision of the state may not impose any mortgage taxes or any sales or transfer taxes on the mortgage or transfer of real property.

ARTICLE XI: GENERAL PROVISIONS

Section 1. The name of this state shall be "North Dakota." The state of North Dakota shall consist of all the territory included within the following boundary, to wit: Commencing at a point in the main channel of the Red River of the North, where the forty-ninth degree of north latitude crosses the same; thence south up the main channel of the same and along the boundary line of the state of Minnesota to a point where the seventh standard parallel intersects the same; thence west along said seventh standard parallel produced due west to a point where it intersects the twenty-seventh meridian of longitude west from Washington; thence north on said meridian to a point where it intersects the forty-ninth degree of north latitude; thence east along said line to place of beginning.

Section 2. The following described seal is hereby declared to be and hereby constituted the great seal of the state of North Dakota, to wit: A tree in the open field, the trunk of which is surrounded by three bundles of wheat; on the right a plow, anvil and sledge; on the left, a bow crossed with three arrows, and an Indian on horseback pursuing a buffalo toward the setting sun; the foliage of the tree arched by a half circle of forty-two stars, surrounded by the motto "Liberty and Union Now and Forever, One and Inseparable"; the words "Great Seal" at the top; the words "State of North Dakota" at the bottom; "October 1st" on the left and "1889" on the right. The seal to be two and one-half inches in diameter.

Section 3. All flowing streams and natural watercourses shall forever remain the property of the state for mining, irrigating and manufacturing purposes.

Section 4. Members of the legislative assembly and the executive and judicial branches, except such inferior officers as may be by law exempted, before they enter on the duties of their respective offices, shall take and subscribe the following oath or affirmation: "I do solemnly swear (or affirm as the case may be) that I will support the Constitution of the United States and the Constitution of the State of North Dakota; and that I will faithfully discharge the duties of the office of _____ according to the best of my ability, so help me God" (if an oath), (under pains and penalties of perjury) if an affirmation, and any other oath, declaration, or test may not be required as a qualification for any office or public trust.

Section 5. Unless otherwise provided by law, all meetings of public or governmental bodies, boards, bureaus, commissions, or agencies of the state or any political subdivision of the state, or organizations or agencies supported in whole or in part by public funds, or expending public funds, shall be open to the public.

Section 6. Unless otherwise provided by law, all records of public or governmental bodies, boards, bureaus, commissions, or agencies of the state or any political subdivision of the state, or organizations or agencies supported in whole or in part by public funds, or expending public funds, shall be public records, open and accessible for inspection during reasonable office hours.

Section 7. The legislative assembly, in order to ensure continuity of state and local governmental operations in periods of emergency resulting from disasters caused by enemy attack, shall have the power and immediate duty

(1) to provide for prompt and temporary succession to the powers and duties of public offices, of whatever nature and whether filled by election or appointment, the incumbents of which may become unavailable for carrying on the powers and duties of such offices, and

(2) to adopt such other measures as may be necessary and proper for ensuring the continuity of governmental operations including, but not limited to, waiver of constitutional restrictions upon the place of transaction of governmental business, upon the calling of sessions of the legislative assembly, length of sessions, quorum and voting requirements, subjects of legislation and appropriation bill requirements, upon eligibility of legislators to hold other offices, residence requirements for legislators, and upon expenditures, loans or donations of public moneys. In the exercise of the powers hereby conferred the legislative assembly shall in all respects conform to the requirements of this constitution except to the extent that in the judgment of the legislative assembly so to do would be impracticable or would admit of undue delay.

Section 8. The house of representatives shall have the sole power of impeachment. The concurrence of a majority of all members elected shall be necessary to an impeachment.

Section 9. All impeachments shall be tried by the senate. When sitting for that purpose the senators shall be upon oath or affirmation to do justice according to the law and evidence. No person shall be convicted without the concurrence of two-thirds of the members elected. When the governor or lieutenant governor is on trial, the presiding judge of the supreme court shall preside.

Section 10. The governor and other state and judicial officers, except county judges, justices of the peace and police magistrates, shall be liable to impeachment for habitual drunkenness, crimes, corrupt conduct, or malfeasance or misdemeanor in office, but judgment in such cases shall not extend further than removal from office and disqualification to hold any office of trust or profit under the state. The person accused, whether convicted or acquitted, shall nevertheless be liable to indictment, trial, judgment and punishment according to law.

Section 11. All officers not liable to impeachment shall be subject to removal for misconduct, malfeasance, crime or misdemeanor in office, or for habitual drunkenness or gross incompetency in such manner as may be provided by law.

Section 12. No officer shall exercise the duties of his office after he shall have been impeached and before his acquittal.

Section 13. On trial of impeachment against the governor, the lieutenant governor shall not act as a member of the court.

Section 14. No person shall be tried on impeachment before he shall have been served with a copy thereof, at least twenty days previous to the day set for trial.

Section 15. No person shall be liable to impeachment twice for the same offense.

Section 16. The reserve militia of this state consists of all able-bodied individuals eighteen years of age and older residing in the state, unless exempted by the laws of the United States or of this state. The active militia is the national guard of this state and consists of individuals who volunteer and are accepted unless exempted by the laws of the United States or of this state. An individual whose religious tenets or conscientious scruples forbid that individual to bear arms may not be compelled to do so in times of peace, but that individual shall pay an equivalent for a personal service.

Section 17. The militia shall be enrolled, organized, uniformed, armed and disciplined in such a manner as shall be provided by law, not incompatible with the constitution or laws of the United States.

Section 18. The legislative assembly shall provide by law for the establishment of volunteer organizations of the several arms of the service, which shall be classed as active militia; and no other organized body of armed men shall be permitted to perform military duty in this state except the army of the United States, without the proclamation of the governor of the state.

Section 19. All militia officers shall be appointed or elected in such a manner as the legislative assembly shall provide.

Section 20. The commissioned officers of the militia shall be commissioned by the governor, and no commissioned officer shall be removed from office except by sentence of court-martial, pursuant to law.

Section 21. The militia forces shall in all cases, except treason, felony or breach of the peace, be privileged from arrest during their attendance at musters, parades and elections of officers, and in going to and returning from the same.

Section 22. The right of the debtor to enjoy the comforts and necessaries of life shall be recognized by wholesome laws, exempting from forced sale to all heads of families a homestead, the value of which shall be limited and defined by law; and a reasonable amount of personal property; the kind and value shall be fixed by law. This section shall not be construed to prevent liens against the homestead for labor done and materials furnished in the improvement thereof, in such manner as may be prescribed by law.

Section 23. The real and personal property of any woman in this state, acquired before marriage, and all property to which she may, after marriage become in any manner rightfully entitled, shall be her separate property, and shall not be liable for the debts of her husband.

Section 24. The labor of children under twelve years of age, shall be prohibited in mines, factories and workshops in this state.

Section 25. The legislative assembly shall not authorize any game of chance, lottery, or gift enterprises, under any pretense, or for any purpose whatever. However, the legislative assembly shall authorize the state of North Dakota to join a multi-state lottery for the benefit of the state of North Dakota, and, the legislative assembly may authorize by law bona fide nonprofit veterans', charitable, educational, religious, or fraternal organizations, civic and service clubs, or such other public-spirited organizations as it may recognize, to conduct games of chance when the entire net proceeds of such games of chance are to be devoted to educational, charitable, patriotic, fraternal, religious, or other public-spirited uses.

Section 26. The legislative, executive, and judicial branches are coequal branches of government. Elected members and officials of each branch shall receive as compensation for their services only such amounts as may be specifically set by law. Payment for necessary expenses shall not exceed those allowed for other state employees.

Section 27. Hunting, trapping, and fishing and the taking of game and fish are a valued part of our heritage and will be forever preserved for the people and managed by law and regulation for the public good.

Section 28. Marriage consists only of the legal union between a man and a woman. No other domestic union, however denominated, may be recognized as a marriage or given the same or substantially equivalent legal effect.

Section 29. The right of farmers and ranchers to engage in modern farming and ranching practices shall be forever guaranteed in this state. No law shall be enacted which abridges the right of farmers and ranchers to employ agricultural technology, modern livestock production, and ranching practices.

ARTICLE XII: CORPORATIONS OTHER THAN MUNICIPAL

Section 1. The term "corporation", as used in this article, does not embrace municipalities or political subdivisions of the state unless otherwise expressly stated.

Section 2. All corporations existing or hereafter chartered hold the charter subject to the provisions of this constitution. The legislative assembly may provide by general laws for the organization and regulation of corporations, and any law, so enacted, is subject to future repeal or amendment.

Section 3. Repealed.

Section 4. Repealed.

Section 5. The exercise of the right of eminent domain shall never be abridged, or so construed as to prevent the legislative assembly from taking the property and franchises of incorporated companies and subjecting them to public use; the same as the property of individuals; and the exercise of the police power of this state shall never be abridged, or so construed as to permit corporations to conduct their business in such a manner as to infringe the equal rights of individuals or the general well-being of the state.

Section 6. Unless otherwise provided in the articles of incorporation, in all elections for directors or managers of a corporation, each member or shareholder may cast the whole number of the member's or shareholder's votes for one candidate, or distribute them upon two or more candidates, as the member or shareholder may prefer, provided, any cooperative corporation may adopt bylaws limiting the voting power of its stockholders.

Section 7. Repealed.

Section 8. Repealed.

Section 9. Repealed.

Section 10. No law shall be passed by the legislative assembly granting the right to construct and operate a street railroad, telegraph, telephone or electric light plant within any city, town or incorporated village, without requiring the consent of the local authorities having the control of the street or highway proposed to be occupied for such purposes.

Section 11. Repealed.

Section 12. Repealed.

Section 13. Repealed.

Section 14. Repealed.

Section 15. Repealed.

Section 16. Any combination between individuals, corporations, associations, or either having for its object or effect the controlling of the price of any product of the soil or any article of manufacture of commerce, or the cost of exchange or transportation, is prohibited and hereby declared unlawful and against public policy; and any and all franchises heretofore granted or extended, or that may hereafter be granted or extended in this state, whenever the owner or owners thereof violate this article shall be deemed annulled and become void.

Section 17. Repealed.

ARTICLE XIII: COMPACT WITH THE UNITED STATES

The following article shall be irrevocable without the consent of the United States and the people of this state:

Section 1. Perfect toleration of religious sentiment must be secured, and no inhabitant of this state may ever be molested in person or property on account of that person's mode of religious worship.

Section 2. Jurisdiction is ceded to the United States over the military reservations of Fort Abraham Lincoln, Fort Buford, Fort Pembina, and Fort Totten, heretofore declared by the president of the United States; provided, legal process, civil and criminal, of this state, extends over those reservations in all cases in which exclusive jurisdiction is not vested in the United States, or of crimes not committed within the limits of those reservations. The legislative assembly may provide, upon the terms and conditions it adopts, for the acceptance of any jurisdiction as may be delegated to the state by act of Congress.

Section 3. The state of North Dakota hereby accepts the several grants of land granted by the United States to the state of North Dakota by an Act of Congress entitled "An act to provide for the division of Dakota into two states, and to enable the people of North Dakota, South Dakota, Montana and Washington to form constitutions and state governments, and to be admitted into the union on equal footing with the original states, and to make donations of public lands to such states," under the conditions and limitations therein mentioned; reserving the right, however, to apply to Congress for modification of said conditions and limitations in case of necessity.

Section 4. All other provisions of the Enabling Act of Congress approved on February 22, 1889, 25 United States Statutes at Large 676, chapter 180, and section 1 of this article of the Constitution of North Dakota, as section 1 existed immediately before the adoption of this section, are continued in effect as though fully recited and continue to be irrevocable without the consent of the United States and the people of this state.

TRANSITION SCHEDULE

Sections 1 to 25. Repealed.

Section 26. The legislative assembly shall provide for the editing, and for the publication in an independent volume, of this constitution as soon as it shall take effect, and whenever it shall be altered or amended, and shall cause to be published in the same volume the Declaration of Independence, the Constitution of the United States and the Enabling Act.

www.ingramcontent.com/pod-product-compliance
Lightning Source LLC
Chambersburg PA
CBHW052339220526
45472CB00001B/494